BLOODRED DRAGONFLIES

By Jim Pascual Agustin
in English and Filipino

Beneath an Angry Star (Anvil Publishing, Manila, 1992)

Salimbayan (Publikasyong Sipat, Manila, 1994)

Baha-bahagdang Karupukan
(University of Santo Tomas Publishing House, Manila, 2011)

Alien to Any Skin (USTPH, Manila, 2011)

Kalmot ng Pusa sa Tagiliran (USTPH, Manila, 2013)

Sound Before Water (USTPH, Manila, 2013)

A Thousand Eyes (USTPH, Manila, 2015)

Sanga sa Basang Lupa at iba pang kuwento (USTPH, Manila, 2016)

Wings of Smoke (The Onslaught Press, Oxford, 2017)

How to Make a Salagubang Helicopter & other poems
(San Anselmo Publications, Quezon City, 2019)

Crocodiles in Belfast & other poems
(San Anselmo Publications, Quezon City, 2020)

Bloodred Dragonflies

New & Selected Poems in English
and Versions from the Filipino

Jim Pascual Agustin

ISBN 978-1-928476-46-7
ebook ISBN 978-1-928476-47-4

Deep South, Makhanda
contact@deepsouth.co.za
www.deepsouth.co.za

Distributed in South Africa by
Blue Weaver Marketing and Distribution
https://blueweaver.co.za

Distributed in the Philippines by
San Anselmo Publications, Inc
marvin.aceron@apvlaw.net

Distributed worldwide by
African Books Collective
PO Box 721, Oxford, OX1 9EN, UK
www.africanbookscollective.com/publishers/deep-south

Deep South would like to thank the National Arts Council
for financially supporting the production of this book

Cover design: Kiara Silayan Agustin
Text design and layout: Liz Gowans

For Kiara, Nina
& Margie

Contents

I

II

III

IV

I

After the First Monsoon Rain

Doors along the narrow line of houses
empty out with children,
banana leaves bend to drop
the last beads of rain down their palms.

He is among them, this boy
with the breath of summer.
The scent of earth roused by rain
fills his lungs.

He runs in zigzags to his friends,
making sure to hit every puddle
with every leap. The louder
the splash, the better.

The Crabs

I was a skinny child, squeamish
about cracking open the crab
my mother cooked. She flinched,
lifting the clumps strung together
from the market, their pincers
bound with bamboo strips.

Their protruding eyes swivelled about,
probing their changed world, their mouths
tiny flapping windows before a brewing
typhoon. Then a frantic banging
on the sides of the pot until
the bubbling drowned them out.

Naartjie

Skin
    winter sunset
    with cloud.
Globe
    fits
    a child's hand
Thumbs
    uncork
    summer.

Decades After the War

You rub your eyes as if in waking. Yet they linger,
threads embedded in your iris. Outlines
of shadows, transparent shapes in a huddle
round the lone water tap. Dusk settles
on the roofs of the school buildings.

You are nine and it is time to go home.
The other kids don't see what makes you tremble,
what makes you feel like you have to pee.
They carry their bags on their shoulders and walk
right through those shapes, as in mist.

Their laughter fades and you are still there,
holding the bottle a teacher asked you to fill.
The uneven ground on the field begins to rise.
The wall of an abandoned fort appears,
calling to the thirsty soldiers.

Seeing in the Dark

it was a gift she never wanted
to use, unless you begged her
for some glimmer of a future

she said faith should be enough
but seeing the doubt in my eyes
she had to allow geometry
to lead me out of the dark

> *you will leave your country*
> *stare loneliness in the eye*
> *bury the dead among the living*
> *and resurrect them unwillingly*
> *because your hands are your way*
> *of seeing in the dark*

i laughed a bitter laughter
i had never heard before

You Had to Leave

Nightmares no longer scare you
like they used to. Not the fat
creature that sits on your chest
before dawn, a pair of new moons
for eyes on a face of darkness.

Not the red hand that touches
your heel, grabs your calf,
drags you under the bed,
your mouth open and soundless.

Not the voice of an old man
mumbling next to your pillow,
then behind the door, then down
the stairs, saying half-words
like air before a downpour.

What you took with you feels
like an open wound
the dogs can smell.

I Don't Ever Wish to Get Used to This

I return from the cold bathroom,
lay my body next to yours
again, still seething
from the flames.

I try to be swept away
by the waves of your slumber.
But light has begun
to flood the room.
Even as I know everything
is new to me, I stare and see
a yellowed photograph.

I turn over, shut my eyes
for stretches of time
under the darkness
of thick blankets,

yet my body knows
the moment of rising
that goes with dawns
past and newly breaking.

The Way a Heart Ricochets

The call of a guinea fowl
in the late hours, a wheel

on an axle that needs oiling,
spun by the wind or a hand

that remains unseen.
Things you never touched

now seem near and distant
at the same time.

The Path of the Wind

for Margie

I have seen days when the wind
weighs so heavy on trees, they bend

close to breaking. A limb
with the greenest leaves

or weakened by age would have to give in.
The trunk may have to learn a new angle

sunward. Less apparent is the path
the wind must make. It has to unravel,

splitting itself into countless strands
to navigate between each leaf, each branch.

Lines Too Late to Utter

Look for me on the edges of shadows
at dusk, away from streetlights
and neons, beyond the urban sprawl
where people are boxed meals.

Listen to my whisper between
a dog's fading howl
and the snapping of a cat's claw
as it runs up a wall
with graffiti skin.

Forget what I wrote you years ago.
Those promises have found
their boundaries. Go, take flight,
my love.

II

Archipelago

From very young it was drummed
in our heads that my country
was an archipelago.
"Think of a man about to lift
a sack of rice," one teacher said.

In high school I saw the shape
of Marcos the dictator and his loot.
Hunched, he boards a US Air Force
helicopter that bends the trees
around the palace grounds
before the mob at the gates break through.

These days it takes the shape of the new tyrant.
His throat, a howling wilderness.
He coughs out curses, splattering them
onto something leaning on his leg,
one more victim bundled up
with packaging tape.

One day I will visit
my homeland again,
as if from outer space,
behold a string of emeralds
on a tilted silver tray.

Dragonflies

It isn't possible to find the old house
where you taught me how to take
my very first steps, Mother.
The government didn't just tear down
its foundations. They buried it
under twenty feet of soil.

Over that, they spread tar
in the name of the dictator,
built a bridge that tore the shoulders
of the river. Then they carved out the hill
that was almost a mountain.

We shook our heads at your tombstone
stretched to the horizon.
The last of the fields
where running children
would freeze in their tracks
at the sight of bloodred dragonflies.

How to Make a Salagubang Helicopter

They prefer mango trees, but any tree
will have at least one. A quick shake
and they fall like pebbles, these beetles,
some still in the act of mating,
glistening with monsoon rain.

One of the bigger boys told me
their prickly legs are harmless,
like thin petals of a flower
opening and closing. "Here,"
he said, handing me one

in the hollow of his fist.
On the lines of my palm,
this salagubang couldn't push
itself upright with the stiff
covers of its wings.

He picked up another beetle,
held it close to my face
and placed index and middle
finger on the grooves of its body.
With the other hand he snapped

off the two kicking back legs.
On their stumps he tied
a thread and on it, with the span
of a hand, knotted a stone.
The salagubang flew

when he let it go, but only
in circles with the stone
dead centre. We laughed.
I could feel the wind
from frantic wings.

Face in the Tar

The dictator's son always got more
than he wished. One birthday it was a yacht
and a man dressed as a baby
leaping out of a giant cake.

One of the dictator's daughters
had a wedding entourage
that rivalled Princess Diana's. The cathedral
would be nothing but rubble afterwards.

The other daughter could have
the face of the moon if she wanted.
The flick of her chin could turn
a teenager into a mangled mess.

The dictator's wife generously grew
a thousand feet just to please the shoes
she was compelled to purchase
to stamp out sadness from her carved out heart.

The dictator himself could make people
disappear from their homes and be found
floating down a river, their heads
athrob with crabs.

If you questioned any of them
your face would be melted into tar
to patch up the highway
that bore his name.

Martial Law Blackout Games

1

Broken rubber sandals were perfect
for a night like this. The adults frozen
by the news on the radio.
The moon a rusty hook.

All we needed was a candle
hidden from view
by our crouching
tightly together.

By the time we had lit
each flimsy rubber strap
hanging on skinny sticks
it would be too late

for the adults to stop us
running in mad laughter
in different directions.
They unleashed shouts and curses.

We didn't know or care
about the consequences
as we scattered droplets
of fire in the dark.

2

Moths the size of our faces
flew low above us. We could strike them
with branches broken
off guava trees.

We didn't need to aim or throw hard.
There were more of them than us.
Our sticks just needed to spin
in the right direction.

So easily they came down in wobbly arcs
and spirals to the ground. We circled one
that fell by the road. Traced with our flashlights
its struggle to get upright.

I felt something like a hand
on my throat at the sight of that trembling
corrugated body, the pattern of brown eyes
on shattered wings.

3

A cousin dared us to see
who could stare the longest
at the lone candle in the middle
of the table.

We held hands, eight of us,
and giggled as if the darkness
around was sticking fingers
in our sides.

Then the mosquitoes began to bite
our legs and arms. Worse,
they buzzed past our eyes.
I was one of the first

to give in to the sting of tears.
The game made us forget
an uncle who hadn't come home
before curfew struck.

Heroes

I saw them
before dawn dissolved
the moon:

stirring coffee
without cups,
fingers with no nails
slowly tapping
a legless table.
seated in the shadows
of kitchen chairs.

Whenever their mouths gaped,
petals broke free,
murmur
of windblown leaves.

Just now,
at the sight of amber
on the acacia trunk
I remember those tales.

Heroes embraced by death
who find no rest
while the stench of war
lingers.

Dawn with Shattered Comb

She scrambled down
the side of the cliff,
her hair a bird flapping
with one wing,
her face caressed
by sea mist.

Low thorny shrubs
scratched her arms,
exposed her legs.
Her tortoiseshell comb
shattered as she tripped,
black jagged stones
cut her feet.

She had fled after the dream
came coiling into her sleep,
turning the stiff sheets
into tentacles.
She reached the dock,
a fist against centuries.
Not a single boat.

As the clouds rolled in,
what she saw approaching
was a continent of skulls.

Escape

The day I visited my nephew
at rehab, there were people
screaming. One of the patients
had bolted when he saw the gate
open. My sister told me to stay
in the vehicle until it was safe.

They caught the guy, beat him up
a bit. Solitary was definite.
My sister unwrapped the food
she packed for all to share,
as if nothing was more ordinary.
The trees gave some shade

that humid afternoon. My nephew said
he'd like to come home again.
All of us knew it wasn't time,
but spoke of days before everything
went dark. Strips of garbage bags
fluttered on the barbed wire.

The Calendar

The state-issued calendar, smooth
and shiny at first, grew a skin
from my mother's cooking,
gathered daily dust and droppings
from geckos.

For years my sisters and I got used
to eating while being watched
by the cardboard eyes of the dictator
and his family, their opulent smiles
mocking the flowerless chalk vases,
the six-inch high bowling trophies,
the scant collection of books
locked behind sliding panels of glass.

Long after the regime was toppled,
my parents still kept the calendar.
They cut off the year and the months,
leaving the picture uneven and jagged.

One day, on coming back from school,
my eyes lingered at a rectangle
on the dining room wall. I saw
a lighter tinge of the same paint,
and holes where the nails had been.

Citizens Military Training

Hand-me-down boots
deep jungle green
a size too big, reeking of memories
of someone else's feet.

Another Saturday morning wasted
pretending to stand at attention
while being spat on
by kitchen-ranked officers.

Suddenly felt something squirm
under my left foot, something under
the thick black sock I had
doubled over to make the boot fit.

This thing resisted the weight
of my toes, pierced through
my sock as if with needles,
made me jump out of line and curse.

Punishment: four hours in full sun.
At long last the stroke of noon,
the relief of loosening laces,
shaking free the boot.

Just then tumbled out, exoskeleton
popped open, a muffled hissing,
a sizzle, a twitch which grew still:
my tormentor, an American cockroach.

Defiance

A streetlamp with a piece of blue wire
sticking out one side. A corner bakery
that lays out a new tray of bread
dusted with fine sugar

an hour before the school bell rings.
An elderly neighbour sweeps
the pavement beyond her property
without ever lifting her head.

Something green, red and brown
hangs off a crumbling ledge,
perhaps a curtain blasted off
a window that overlooked

a busy street I used to roam.
Someone I knew who once waved
from that window, hoping
I would wave back.

Quiet Light

You can almost hear them bridging breaths
between whispers, stifling joy on the verge
of laughter to keep in time with quiet light.

Though they are framed in the regions
of almost-forgetting, there is a muted
throbbing in what they touch: a trinket box,

the tips of flowers and leaves, a letter suffused
with light and secrets, hand-polished shells
nestled in the hollows of a paused game of *sungka*.

You can almost touch the embroidery
on their clothes, kindred spirits
taking their time in passing.

We Will Not Allow the Dead to be Silenced

The man who curses shall be cursed
to live forever in the stories we shall tell
our children. They will not fear him
or his twisted reincarnations.

Our children shall not be shaken
by his threats. His attack dogs
with teeth of bullets will not make us
turn away and flee.

Though the dead may be left
unclaimed in morgues
or dumped on the side of the road,
their faces bound with packaging tape,

they will never be silenced.
The veins on their exposed necks
and stiffened arms will turn to roots.
And we who fight to remember

the cruelty inflicted upon
those we can no longer hold
shall bear bitter fruit
to be shoved down the tyrant's throat.

Birthday Wish for a Dictator

Your birthday disturbs me.
It is far too close to mine
and to the brother I gained and lost,
the one who glimpsed the cavern

where I kept a cauldron of stones
the size of heads, each one
carved with your name. Yes,
there have been others worse

than you, and doubtless more
will follow in your wake.
But today I celebrate
that hate is not why I breathe.

The Dogs of the Children Who Died of Sadness

for the people of the Chagos Islands

Monsters came one day, dressed
in stiff uniforms. Fed largely
on red meat, they had grown
like giants compared to the islanders.

They scarred the land as they drove,
engines growling like hungry beasts,
churning sand and dust into the terrified
eyes of the children. Their small
brown arms grew powerless.

Never before had they seen such nightmares.
The monsters had come to gather all
the dogs of the island. They took them away
amid cries and screams.

III

Rats

My father said I'd been lucky to grow up
with neither famine nor war.

"What's it like to eat rat?"
"If cooked right, they taste almost like chicken."

"What about the fur? The snout?
The tail? The little feet, the fingers?"

Father's stare cut right through me
as if in search of something
running and hiding among the foliage.

The veins on his neck grew
visible, the bones in his hands
leapt with the momentary jerk.

All of a sudden I grew cold,
swept away by a world
I did not wish to see.

Thirty Years After

He was just an old man
with a cane and a bad aim.
We taunted him
with our noise.

All the children knew
when he opened his mouth
there'd be a sudden smell
of warm earth after a downpour.

His voice hovered between
rasp of dry leaves
and snap of brittle branches.

Even when he was quiet,
his long fingers still on the thick
wooden ledge, we felt
the weight of his eyes
slowing down our marbles game.

Those unstable legs once took him
through jungle and hostile countryside
in a time of war, to get my mother
to safety. Or so I'm told
thirty years after his passing.

The Taste of War

Salt came from the shops
in dull plastic bags, then decanted
in a jar that was rarely washed.
Bottles of vinegar, *patis* and soy sauce
stood side by side on a wooden shelf.
Under them, containers for sugar and coffee
emptied from sachets, and a single box
of matches. These were her riches.

Having lost her childhood and her mother
in the war, she taught herself
how to cook. But how does one fend off
the lingering taste of war
with the barest spices?
The lash of *talahib* on skinny legs may fade
along with the memory of running
into the jungle to escape patrolling soldiers.

But her hands recalled
how they hunted smaller creatures
for food before nightfall.
How her small fists desperately tried to silence
crushing hunger. How her parched mouth
stifled cries at the sight of people
turning into limp rags
as they were struck with bayonets.

Years later, as she cut the head off
a chicken, as she gutted a fish,
did she recall the taste of violence?

Bladed Spurs

They lived in bamboo cages
under the house. They heard
our footsteps on the wooden floor,
felt the dust coming down like rain

between the slats. They must have
regularly heard my mother screaming
in a bad dream, my sisters fighting
over a hairbrush or a shirt, my father

cursing at a missed hoop shot
on TV. But they never heard me.
When I came down to feed them
scoops of mixed grain in water

with my bare hands, their eyes
were shifty. As alert as when
they are about to be thrown
in the middle of a sandy ring,

the shouts of jostling men
in tiers of wood and concrete
around them, closing in
with bets and spits,

where death awaited in beaks
and bladed spurs. My father would
sometimes tell me to hold one
of them as he trimmed down

its comb. "It covers an eye
when it flops down too long,"
he explained, "a handicap
in a fight." The rooster's heart

beat against my hands,
the heat of skin
beneath its feathers
burned with a metallic shine.

My Father, Leaving

the last words i heard from you
were not words at all

the chemicals in your body
were clawing at your veins

invisible knives were stabbing you,
or merciless angels were forcing

the sharp ends of feathers
into your yellowing back

yellow like the bare skin
of your fighting cocks

that made it back home
limp

static on the phone line, your cries,
words that were not words

Consuelo Garcia, Please Stop

Consuelo Garcia, please stop inviting my mother
to join you for a walk. She can barely shift
her weight in the chair or on the bed.

There are strangers who keep entering
her room uninvited, not uttering
a word to her, just standing around.
She shoos them away, desperately

asking them to leave her alone.
There are even unknown children
who climb into her bed, sitting
and staring at her. I don't know how

she sees them when cataracts
have clouded her eyes for years now.
I'm not there to soothe
my mother's fears.

Consuelo Garcia, I'm asking you,
if you can hear me half a world away,
please do something. Weren't you
her close friend? My sister says
you passed away a decade ago. Please go.

Hands Over Face

any day now
the sky will turn liquid
all engines will be silenced
hands in a casket

my grandfather mumbled these words
before he stared forever
they made no sense
yet i still remember them

i remember being small
and the ceiling white, immense
mother ran her hands over
grandfather's face, as if she were blind

her fingers drew down his eyelids
but in my mind he kept
staring right through
the ceiling

nine weeks later i heard the sounds
he used to make
while searching for his slippers,
dark leather and stone heavy

or maybe for his *yantok* cane,
that third leg, that third arm
he used to wield at neighbours'
children who stole guavas from his yard

or searching for the key to his door
that he'd grown too frail to shut
and any moment now
he will call on us   one of us   me

The Call

The last time we saw each other,
clouds hadn't yet settled over your eyes.
My sisters, for all their love,
kept sending photographs of you
as if everything would go on forever
like the inescapable fog you grew to accept.
Still, in a handful of photos, you smile
without a trace of pain.

When it was time for you to go,
I was on the other side of the world,
sawing off branches high up a tree
whose shallow roots clung
to drought-stricken ground.
Metal teeth had struck my arm
and I had to climb down to go inside.
That's when the phone rang.

Letter Never Written by My Father

Son, I promise not to be an unwelcome visitor.
If I find my way to your house,
I won't be a bother. I promise not to touch the door,
or press my ears against the walls to hear
the slow breathing of your twin daughters.

I'll be the familiar silence between
the coughing sounds from a stranger.
You might see the pattern of my left palm
in the exposed veins of a leaf.
A swift wind might give your collar
a tug, as I once did.

When You Turned Transparent

There was no resistance
when you loosened your skin,
unbuttoned flesh from bones,

slipped them off until you turned
transparent as water, shapeless
and silent, light through fog.

You got up and left without a sound.
No one saw you walk through
the unseen door which opens

to somewhere else.
I hope you can read this in that place
where you can now laugh

without doubling over. I'm glad
the last thing that touched your lips
was a thin slice of pink guava.

The Letter

After reading it once more
(lost count of the times),
I hold it against a fiercer light.
The words interweave
on either side of the sheet.
I can no longer tell what's written.
But lay it down on the table,
letting light strike it as it should,
the words return:
weight of black ink
carved on yellow paper.

Angels of the Old Cemetery

Some haven't fallen completely
to ruin. A few fingers snapped
off, a nose chipped, a wing lopped
to the ground by a loitering teen,
Or just gravity finding the weak
points of aged concrete.

They remain standing
on weathered pillars or lying
on the ground with arms pointing
at the sky, having forgotten the names
of the bodies they were meant
to watch over, the souls
they were to guide
from the wood and the soil.

What I've Always Been

Call it aging, or what perhaps
I've always been,

someone who loses and gains
all the time. Not seeming to care

or able to see an oncoming train
on its side, the ground grating

against its metal skin, screams
twisting on the tracks. And my eyes

not flinching
still staring in the distance.

IV

Chameleon Birth

Veins pulsing, she grips
the branch that holds her up.
Tongue bunched inside
her jaws, soundless. Her slit
of flesh finally blossoms,

a ball of slime drops but refuses
to plunge to rough ground.
Membrane clings to closest
branch. In a breath, a limb
breaks that soft sheet

and this thing, a minuscule version
of its mother, starts to climb. Born
with the same slumbering
acrobatic agility, it creeps upward,
seeks warmth for its fragile skin

while she gives birth to another
and another. Until, all life
nearly drained, she heads down.
Slow body gently presses
against each offspring,
a first and last caress.

How the Pineapple Came to Be

The mother sought to share the burden of chores.
The child preferred to twist and stretch
time in her little mind. The mother kept
asking her daughter to find a broom, a pot,
a ladle, or something else dictated
by domestic life. Her voice grew dry
as overcooked rice.

"I cannot find it, mother," was Pina's
repeated reply while snapping spiderwebs.
 "Use your eyes, my child,
or may you have a thousand!"

Those were the last words she heard
from her mother. The curse
unleashed in half a breath,
struck Pina's dreaming head.
Then there was silence
heavy as nightfall on an empty bed.

A mother's grief, a village search
until dawn. With countless eyes
wide and unseeing, Pina stared
forever at her mother
doubled over at the bottom
of the wooden steps.

The Wind is Not Strong Enough
to Slam the Windows Shut

He roams a wilderness in his head,
the way an astrophysicist,
wary of drowning in darkness,
might navigate numbers
to reach a point in space.

The veins on the back of his hands
are roots that quiver when his heart
quickens. It's a struggle to sleep,
a struggle to stay awake.

A neighbour's donkey
cranks out a mechanical cry.
He is reminded of empty chairs,
of sheets on another bed
bearing shadows and creases.

The Sound Before Water

for Cristina Pantoja Hidalgo

the sound just before water
reaches the end
of a tap when you are

about to wash your hands
is not much different
from that deep breath

you take in before diving
but you don't hear it
because it is not your breath

and no one thinks of diving
at that moment when hands
need washing

unless your mind takes you
to a bridge in fog
or a boat without oars

or a miscounted step
on the stairs you thought you knew
with your eyes closed

not everyone
has a tap
not everyone
disappears forever
into fog, or is embraced

by deep waters, falling
when they expected
someone's arms

Trace Me

"Trace me," she whispers in the glow
of communion, intense and feeble.
The waves inaudible
behind sliding glass doors.

This thirst, this assertion.
This painful moving towards each other's
lost longing, amid the rush
of lives around us.

I lift a finger. Slow as a snail
on the verge of a leaf,
linger where skin
begins to glisten.

The Scar Examined at Midnight

tell me about that. that scar.

it is a burn. something has grown
over it that mimics skin.
feel.

my memory goes blurry
when you smoke.
i know you need to, but please don't.
or i won't tell you the story.

it is not a burn.
more like a reminder.
like some people write notes
to themselves,

stick them next to doorknobs
so as not to forget
something they must take
before leaving.

i threw my arms around a woman
who wanted to leap into the fire.
but it was too late.
we held each other too late.

tell me about that.
yes, tell me about that.

Stay a Minute

What I remember:
sunlight framed by a window
with broken glass
just before night says

"Now, it is I who will touch
your hands without permission."
Nothing can make me forget
the warmth, my own breath

an approaching train, the beating
of an iron heart. No one will believe me
when what is broken doesn't show
even the thinnest crack.

Night Driving in Fog

moving in nothing
but thick white
that caves in around us

the awkward meal
dirty dishes, hosts
blurring away

right headlight scrapes
gravel, the left
holds up ghosts

not a trace
of the arched branches
on the scenic drive in

between us, the stiff handbrake

you press the dashboard
like a stranger coming
too close

any moment now
visible air could turn
into concrete
or steel

The Scorch on the Asphalt

The car in front
two seconds ahead of mine
struck him head-on.

Two years since the day
the sun scorched his blood
onto the asphalt,
a trapped ghost.

It's still there, close to the island
on the highway, a dark shape
stretched on a darker surface.
Invisible to other drivers.

Song of My Dark Hour

I'd seen many photographs of her,
all blurred and discoloured.
Whoever took them must have struggled
to focus on so many faces.

"It is easier to remember
the old country this way,"
she once told me. I didn't lift my head
from the light of my cell phone.

"One day you will be like my mother,"
she said, "unable to hold anything
in her own hands, like I'll be soon."
We used to hug, I remember,

but now I find myself turning away,
afraid of the lines on her face,
much like the patterns of nautilus shells
left on a beach no one visits.

Your Own Body, a Universe

You were once like water,
nearly impossible to contain.
If anyone smiled,
laughter would burst out of you
like a spring between boulders.

Sorrow tugged you inward,
but you left a coiled end
like the string of a toy boat
in the bath, something for us to hold,
to pull you past ripples,
until you reached shore.

You're now at the age when
the chemicals in your body are waging war,
and your body itself is a universe
yet to be charted, a devouring world
that grows more alien each day.
All our attempts to reach you
end with the slamming of doors.

The vessel that carries your soul
goes wayward. It flares up
and discharges bombs
at random. Sometimes a black hole
pulls you in. You swirl
among constellations, beyond embrace.

These days, the house
is an abandoned ship.
Ghosts roam the decks.
But we're still certain
that one day we'll hear
laughter from a distant galaxy.

Subway, Rondebosch

A warning in the subway
from a big woman:
"If they ask for money
just walk on."

I had to ask her twice
what she meant. She said it
again with the same cold
voice, sharp

glance towards the stairs
she had just descended.
It was dark underground.

Light and shadow
jagged the way.
The metal railing felt like
deep frozen meat.

Five steps before ground level
I saw two men,
eyes waiting.

They had heard the woman.
Their lips were heavy with words
unuttered. They wore jackets.

In my mind
something double-edged
was being drawn.
I turned around.

The Undiminished

A hurried meal
of last night's leftovers, a shared
cup of tea, then a dash to join
others who wait in line

for a taxi packed beyond capacity.
Always, the unavoidable
pressing of skin against skin, sharing
the scent of familiar strangers.

An eternity to get to work. Time
is a wall that watches our every move.
The journey back even longer. The dark
melts around us, our feet stick

to the concrete. Almost shadows, we fight
our way home, our limbs aching
for the arms of those who seek
the undiminished glimmer in our eyes.

Salagubang

I was reading a book
from England
when something rattled
on the window. *Salagubang*.

Its chocolate-coloured wings
partly showing, it clung
to the tiny squares
of the screen. The moment

I came close, it slowly hid
its wings, like a secret.
Its body quivered,
as if panting

after a long journey.
Miracle of terraced fragility,
it climbed up
a few squares

before it ceased
and seemed to stare
at me and the book
in my hand.

The floor, the window,
the whole room, everything
was floating
in this ancient stare.

Various Histories

The Philippines is an archipelago of over 7,000 islands, so taking to the water has been a necessity and a skill among its inhabitants. Its geographic location made it a natural trading post in the Pacific long before the first Europeans arrived in their galleons. It also sits on major earthquake fault lines and is part of the chain of active volcanoes around Asia known as the Ring of Fire. Typhoons regularly visit the country, often leaving huge devastation.

My country of birth has had a long list of invaders through the centuries. The colonial empire of Spain ruled with cross and sword for over 300 years. The United States of America, in its roughly 50 years of domination, introduced the public education system along with torture and genocide. Japan staked its bayonets for three years during World War II.

In the late 1890s, Philippine revolutionaries were fighting to put an end to Spanish rule. The Spanish knew they no longer had the power to keep the country, but they could not admit defeat to people they deemed to be unworthy opponents. America was waiting at the doorstep, laying the foundations for its young empire. It earned the trust of revolutionary leaders by promising to support their new government. A mock battle was staged in Manila Bay in May 1898 between the two colonial powers with Spain "surrendering" to the Americans. But within months this became reality when the Treaty of Paris was signed, declaring Spain's defeat and the agreement to sell the Philippines for $20 million to the USA.

It was in those turbulent years that Filipino crew members on trade ships passing the coast of Cape Town decided to abandon their posts and stay ashore. They established the first fishing community in Kalk Bay. When I first got here I thought I would be the first Filipino to set foot in South Africa. Much later I learned how inaccurate that was.

I arrived in South Africa in October 1994 knowing only one person. I had met her on my first trip to the Mountain Province in the Philippines in 1993. She was on holiday from teaching English in Japan. She did not have the luckiest time in Manila, losing her travellers cheques soon after arriving. Someone suggested she go up north. We were both trying to catch a bus from Banaue (home of famous rice terraces) that would take us to Bontoc and Sagada. The bus was already full of locals, so we ended up riding on the roof for the hours-long drive on narrow roads right next to cliffs. Being the monsoon season, the roads were slippery with mud and we were told a number of times to jump off the side away from the sheer drop below if the vehicle began to tilt. The shared adventure brought us together. She came back to live with me in Manila the following year, then I followed her to South Africa.

I didn't know back then that Cape Town would become my home. Each time a stranger approached me – often not in a friendly way – they assumed I was from somewhere else. My appearance somehow drew anti-Chinese remarks. To those who showed real interest rather than veiled animosity, I tried to explain where I came from by identifying nearby countries like Thailand and Malaysia.

****

I lost both grandfathers when I was very young. I remember very little about them. My mother's father lived in a room upstairs that had wide windows made of *capiz* – translucent, flattish shells from a particular type of oyster, cut to fit small squares in a wooden grid. I remember light coming in even when he shut those windows. He had a violin in the corner of the room, but he never took it out of the case. He had been a young widower taking care of three daughters and a son during the Japanese invasion in World War II. There are photographs of me as a toddler sitting in his lap, a rare smile for the camera. He barely spoke to us, but with a single shout he would send the neighbours' kids running, dropping the guavas they tried to steal.

My father would have gone to university on a scholarship for his soccer playing abilities, but he had to support the studies of his younger sister. Military service seemed a good option, so he joined the Philippine Air Force. When he got called to duty, he would disappear for days. We were never told to where, for what. He claimed he was related to the Marcoses, coming from the same province in the north, and that they shared a middle name.

My mother was a public school teacher. She got up at five each morning to prepare food for the whole family before setting off on foot to the local primary school. Many years after she retired, her former students would visit our house with Christmas offerings, sometimes with their young families in tow.

My parents were active members of a local community organisation which called itself "Land for the Landless" – people who put up their own houses and looked after their own needs on land outside the reach of government services. It was a rural area on the outskirts of Manila with rice fields and small vegetable farms by the river.

We lived in a house that had been expanded many times through the decades to accommodate our extended family. Rooms were added or split up with thin dividers, sometimes just with blankets. Cousins and their own growing families somehow managed to make space. The whole house was a patchwork, with new wood nailed against thick old trunks.

In the late 1970s, the Marcoses wanted to build a highway, naming it after the dictator. Our house stood in the way, as did most of the houses in the community. One day huge machinery arrived, dumping mountains of soil and gravel. My family was paid a measly sum and given a short deadline to move out. The top part of our house was lifted off its base by volunteers and loaded onto the back of a truck which took it a few kilometres down to a new spot. At one point it got stuck on a low hanging power cable. One of the neighbours climbed to the roof to deal with it. He got electrocuted and was rushed to the hospital. Relatives took over our house in that new location, and my family moved to another part of town. Soon grey concrete roads buried the remaining rice paddies in the area. In the regime of Ferdinand E. Marcos the Philippines, once South East Asia's economic wonder, became the country with the worst foreign debt record in the region.

When martial law was declared in 1972, I was a toddler. Curfews remained in force as I grew up – the hushed talk of the adults about protests, arrests and disappearances went on for many years. My parents were Marcos loyalists, the quiet type who didn't join campaign rallies and believed every word from the government-controlled media. The Marcos family and their cronies took over major businesses and independent media entities. They buried the population in debt while putting on an extravagant show of wealth. The military crushed all dissent and resistance. In 1983 the assassination of Ninoy Aquino, the staunchest critic of the regime, galvanised the opposition. There were protest rallies in different parts of the country, even in the conservative business districts.

Marcos declared there would be snap elections in early February 1986, to prove to the country that he remained popular. Cory Aquino, the widow of Ninoy, became the unlikely candidate for the opposition. My mother, like all public school teachers, was required to work at the polls. As she oversaw the manual counting of ballots which went on through the night, she knew that the Marcos administration had lost. It made her cry in disbelief. In many parts of the country there were reports of violence at the polls, of election officials resisting armed men who wanted to snatch ballot boxes.

During the national counting of votes it became clear the Marcos regime had tried to rig the elections. Cory Aquino called for nationwide civil disobedience. Former military supporters of Marcos declared a coup to oust him, and the Catholic Church sent out a call for people to protect them. Huge numbers responded, filling the major streets and highways of the capital. Fighter jets were sent to threaten them. Tanks rolled down the streets, but people blocked them with their own bodies. The few soldiers who still supported Marcos had running battles with the soldiers who had joined the coup. The military was ordered to fire at the protesters – they refused. Although under siege, the Marcoses declared victory and used state television to broadcast a flag-waving event, but within hours they were airlifted from the presidential palace by US Forces and brought to Hawaii. Soon afterwards, protesters broke through the gates. The groundswell of popular support swept Cory Aquino to the presidency in what would be called the 1986 People Power Revolution.

School was called off just before the elections. I was a high school student then, awkward and out of place in the exclusive Ateneo de Manila run by Jesuits, where I had been accepted on a financial scholarship. Some of my classmates had joined rallies. I never dared. But in February 1986, I took a jeepney as far as I could, then went on foot to join thousands of people ambling about on EDSA, the widest road in Manila, as if they were in a fiesta. I walked with them for hours, past buildings pitted with bullet holes, and corners where flowers and rosaries had been offered to soldiers.

I couldn't tell my family where I'd been. My father finally came home after being holed up in the military base. He was incensed because he had to buy yellow ribbons (the colour of the opposition) and tie them to his vehicle to be let through the crowds. He and my mother wept together. In the space of a few days he had lost all his authority. During martial law anyone could get picked up by a soldier or a lowly police officer for the slightest reason. Growing up with a father in the military gave my family a sense of protection. He was often called upon by relatives to help get someone out of trouble.

Under the Marcos regime all senior high school and first year university students were required to undergo citizens military training. We were told we could be called to serve any time to fight the growing insurgency. The new government that took over didn't remove this policy. I had no money to buy army boots. I got hand-me-downs, two sizes too big. I had to wear thick socks and fold them over. I broke my ankle once running with those oversized boots. We had drills every Saturday morning until noon. One time we were ordered to be at a military base to learn to fire a rifle. That day my best friend got kicked in the side by one of the soldiers for laughing when we were supposed to be aiming at targets.

After the death in exile of the former dictator, the Marcos family were allowed to return to the country. They refused to return the funds they had stolen while they were in power. They never recognised nor apologised for the human rights abuses committed under the dictatorship. They regained their foothold in politics in both local and national elections.

The outgoing president of the Philippines, Rodrigo Duterte, elected in 2016, is facing possible arrest by the International Criminal Court for his so-called War on Drugs during which between 7,000 and 30,000 have been killed – not just accused drug users but also political and environmental activists, indigenous people, lawyers, mayors, church leaders, and journalists. Before he came to power, the country had seen an economic boom under the leadership of the son of Cory Aquino, Benigno Aquino Jr. All those gains were squandered by the rampant corruption that Duterte and his officials orchestrated.

In early 2022, just when this book was being printed, the former dictator's son, Ferdinand Marcos Jr, was running for president. His main opponent was Leni Robredo, who, like Cory Aquino, is the widow of a prominent political leader. Robredo had previously beaten Marcos Jr when they both ran for vice president of the country. She promised to end impunity and corruption.

Notes

p.11 "After the First Monsoon Rain" – The monsoon rains, *Habagat* (Southwest monsoon) and *Amihan* (Northeast monsoon), used to bring bounty and joy to children in the Philippines. These days the rains are something to dread – because of climate change, they bring deluge and destruction like never before.

p.14 "Decades After the War" – The public primary school I attended had a series of massive rocks imbedded in the open area where the students gathered for school assemblies. Some rocks were remains of the walls of a military outpost for Japanese soldiers during WWII. Whether this was true or not mattered little to young minds.

p.24 "How to Make a Salagubang Helicopter" – The *salagubang* is a common beetle, brown and unremarkable, which used to arrive with the change of seasons. It has become a rare sight in Manila; even harder to find now are its more spectacular varieties in metallic green or gold called *salaguinto*.

p.26 "Face in the Tar" – The gruesome details in the poem are no exaggeration.

p.36 "Quiet Light" – This was inspired by the paintings by Celeste Lecaroz of women in clothes dating back to Spanish rule. *Sungka* is a game played on a boat-shaped board that has seven holes on either side, each filled with seven shells (seeds or stones may also do), and two big holes on each end which serve as respective "homes" for each player. It is a game of speed and mathematical calculation.

p.40 "The Dogs of the Children Who Died of Sadness" – The people of the Chagos Islands were forcibly removed by the British government from 1968 to 1973 to make way for the United States to establish a military base in the middle of the Indian Ocean. They remain refugees in Mauritius and the Seychelles.

p.45 "The Taste of War" – *Patis* is fish sauce and *talahib* is the common tall grass.

p.46 "Bladed Spurs" – Cock fighting was introduced by the Spanish. Roosters were introduced from colonies in other parts of the world. It is a ruthless pastime, usually reserved for men.

p.62 "How the Pineapple Came to Be" – This is a retelling of a Philippine myth told to all young children as a warning about being lazy.

p.68 "Stay a Minute" – This poem draws from a scene in "Red," the final film of the trilogy "Three Colours" by the late Polish director Krzysztof Kieślowski.

p.73 "Song of My Dark Hour" – This was written after a photograph by Paul I. Tañedo for a book project that remains as a work in progress.

p.75 "The Undiminished" – This is based on a black and white photograph of workers in half-light by Richelle Belingon, a young photographer in the Philippines.

p.61 "Chameleon Birth" – This was inspired by the documentary "Life in Cold Blood" by David Attenborough.

Acknowledgements

Earlier versions of some of the poems in this book were published in my previous books and in the following journals and anthologies. Some are translations of poems from my books in Filipino. Titles of some poems have been revised.

Journals:

Aerodrome, New Coin, PoetryNet/Litnet, Sixfold, Our Own Voice

Blogs and websites:

AVBOB poetry, my blog *Matangmanok*

Anthologies and other publications:

Off the Beaten Track
(National Book Development Board, 2010)

In the Heat of Shadows: South African Poetry 1996-2013
(Deep South, 2014)

Happiness: The Delight-Tree
(United Nations, 2015)

Dialogo: An Art Monograph of the paintings of Celeste Lecaroz
(San Anselmo Publications, 2021).

Printed in the United States
by Baker & Taylor Publisher Services